Dinosaurs and Prehistoric Animals

Woolly Mammoth

by Helen Frost

Consulting Editor: Gail Saunders-Smith, PhD

Consultant: Jack Horner
Curator of Paleontology
Museum of the Rockies
Bozeman, Montana

Capstone press

Mankato, Minnesota

Pebble Plus is published by Capstone Press,
151 Good Counsel Drive, P.O. Box 669, Mankato, Minnesota 56002.
www.capstonepress.com

1 2 3 4 5 6 10 09 08 07 06 05

Library of Congress Cataloging-in-Publication Data
Frost, Helen, 1949–
    Woolly mammoth / by Helen Frost.
    p. cm.—(Pebble plus—dinosaurs and prehistoric animals)
    Includes bibliographical references and index.
    ISBN 0-7368-3649-7 (hardcover)
    ISBN 0-7368-5109-7 (paperback)
    1. Woolly mammoth—Juvenile literature. I. Title. II. Series.
QE882.P8F76 2005
569'.67—dc22   2004011093

Summary: Simple text and illustrations present woolly mammoths, their body parts, and behavior.

Editorial Credits
Martha E. H. Rustad, editor; Linda Clavel, designer; Jon Hughes, illustrator; Wanda Winch, photo researcher;
  Scott Thoms, photo editor

Photo Credit
Yukon Beringia Interpretive Centre, 21

The author thanks the children's library staff at the Allen County Public Library in Fort Wayne, Indiana,
for research assistance.

Note to Parents and Teachers

The Dinosaurs and Prehistoric Animals set supports national science standards related
to the evolution of life. This book describes and illustrates woolly mammoths. The
images support early readers in understanding the text. The repetition of words and
phrases helps early readers learn new words. This book also introduces early readers
to subject-specific vocabulary words, which are defined in the Glossary section. Early
readers may need assistance to read some words and to use the Table of Contents,
Glossary, Read More, Internet Sites, and Index sections of the book.

Table of Contents

A Big Hairy Mammal

Woolly mammoths
were big mammals.
They looked like
hairy elephants.

Woolly mammoths lived

in prehistoric times.

They lived about 500,000

years ago in cold parts

of the world.

How Woolly Mammoths Looked

Woolly mammoths were
as tall as a basketball hoop.
They stood about 10 feet
(3 meters) tall.

Woolly mammoths
had two long tusks.
They may have used
their tusks for fighting.

Woolly mammoths
had long brown fur.
The fur kept them warm.

What Woolly Mammoths Did

Woolly mammoths
used their long trunks
to eat and drink.

Woolly mammoths
ate grass and leaves.
They chewed their food
with wide, flat teeth.

The End of Woolly Mammoths

People may have hunted
woolly mammoths.
People may have built huts
with woolly mammoth bones.

Woolly mammoths died out
about 9,000 years ago.
No one knows why they
all died. You can see
woolly mammoth fossils
in museums.

21

Glossary

elephant—a large mammal that lives in Africa and India; elephants have long trunks and ivory tusks.

fossil—the remains or traces of an animal or a plant, preserved as rock

hunt—to chase and kill animals for food or sport

museum—a place where interesting objects of art, history, or science are shown

prehistoric—very, very old; prehistoric means belonging to a time before history was written down; dinosaurs and sabertooth cats are other prehistoric animals.

trunk—the long nose of a woolly mammoth or an elephant

tusk—one of a pair of long, pointed teeth of a woolly mammoth, an elephant, or a walrus

Read More

Arnold, Caroline. *When Mammoths Walked the Earth.* New York, Clarion, 2002.

Goecke, Michael P. *Woolly Mammoth.* Prehistoric Animals. A Buddy Book. Edina, Minn.: Abdo, 2003.

Hehner, Barbara. *Ice Age Mammoth: Will This Ancient Giant Come Back to Life?* New York: Crown Publishers, 2001.

Miller, Debbie S. *A Woolly Mammoth Journey.* Boston: Little, Brown, 2001.

Internet Sites

FactHound offers a safe, fun way to find Internet sites related to this book. All of the sites on FactHound have been researched by our staff.

Here's how:

1. Visit *www.facthound.com*

2. Type in this special code **0736836497** for age-appropriate sites. Or enter a search word related to this book for a more general search.

3. Click on the **Fetch It** button.

FactHound will fetch the best sites for you!

Index

body parts, 10,
    14, 16

bones, 18

died out, 20

drink, 14

eat, 14, 16

fighting, 10

food, 16

fossils, 20

fur, 12

habitat, 6

hunted, 18

mammals, 4

museums, 20

people, 18

prehistoric, 6

size, 8

teeth, 16

trunks, 14

tusks, 10

warm, 12

Word Count: 132
Grade Level: 1
Early-Intervention Level: 14